The Difference Between Dogs, Wolves, Foxes and Hyenas

Children's Science & Nature

BABY PROFESSOR

EDUCATION KIDS

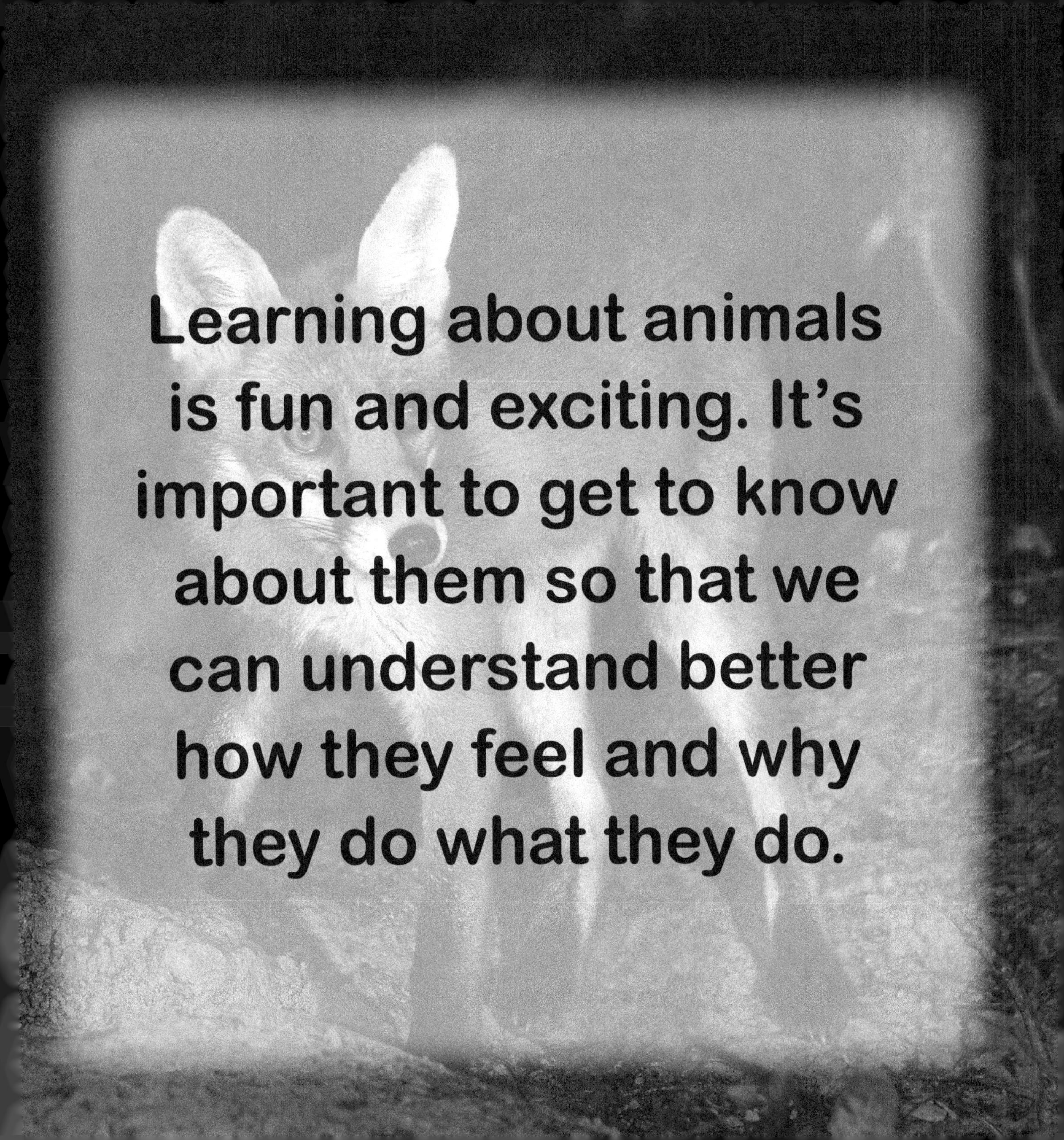

Learning about animals is fun and exciting. It's important to get to know about them so that we can understand better how they feel and why they do what they do.

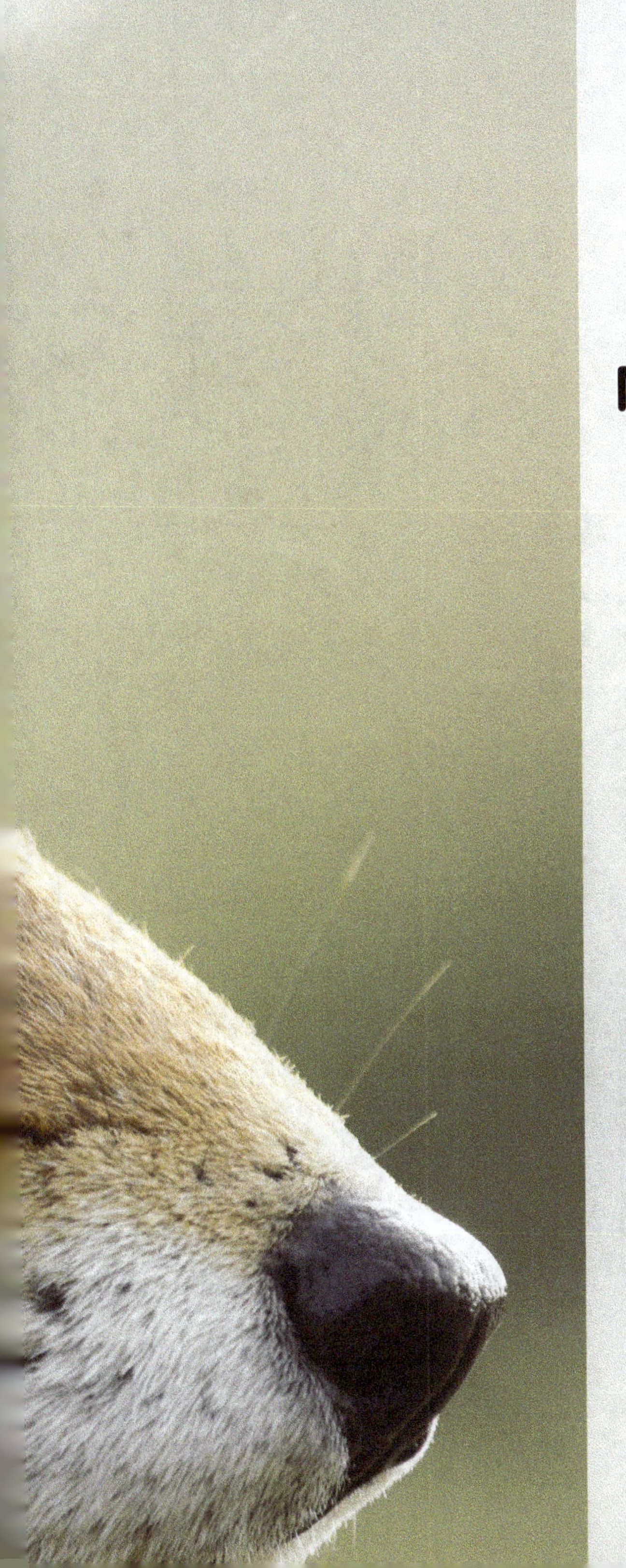

The Canidae Family. Members of the Canidae family are called "canids". Most canids hunt their food and eat other animals. Some canids are scavengers, while a few feed on plants. They have large jaws and teeth. Canids can run fast. They have a good sense of hearing and smell.

The Fennec fox is
the smallest in the
Canidae family while
the gray wolf is the
largest. The Canidae
family is composed of
coyotes, dogs, foxes,
jackals, and wolves

DOGS. Dogs are considered to be man's best friend. They have lived with humans for thousands of years. They are the most popular pets. Dogs descended from wolves. Interestingly, out pet dogs are related to the fierce and wild wolves.

Dogs were believed to be tamed over 12,000 years ago. All dogs belong to the canine or canidae family. Dogs are our adorable pets at home. They can be trained and can be taught many tricks. They are smart animals. The only dog that can climb trees is called the raccoon dog. It resembles a raccoon.

Dogs run fast and they have strong muscles. They can walk on their toes. Dogs have amazing senses of hearing and smell. In fact, dogs can smell more than 100,000 times better than we can and can hear ten times better than humans.

Dogs bark, yelp, whine, and growl to communicate. Chocolate is dangerous for dogs. You should not let your pet dogs eat chocolate. It would make them sick and could kill them. Chocolate contains theobromine. It's a poison to dogs.

There are different types and breeds of dogs. They come in different sizes. Some are big while others are small. Dogs perform different functions. Some of them do police work and hunting, or help herd sheep. Their intelligence makes them a great companion for people.

WOLVES. Are you afraid of wolves? Did you know that humans and wolves are very similar? Wolves live with their families. They live in packs. Each pack has a female or male leader. The leader is called the Alpha Wolf. Only the Alphas have babies. As the leader, the Alpha gives hunting directions. They also solve conflicts within the packs. All members of the pack will take care of the baby wolves, the pups.

Wolves are meat eaters, or carnivores. They eat deer, moose, rabbits, mice and many other animals. They hunt large animals in teams. Wolves howl to communicate with the other wolves. Wolves love to play with one another. When they play, they wrestle and pretend to bite each other!

FOXES. Foxes are members of the dog family. They are nocturnal, which means they are active at night. They are most popular in North America and the United Kingdom.

Foxes are bigger than
a cat and can live up to
14 years. A female fox is
known as a vixen while
the male is called a dog.
A baby fox is called a cub.

Foxes live in a den, known as an earth. They eat worms, spiders, berries, bread, eggs and many other foods. They usually hide their food to be eaten at a later time.

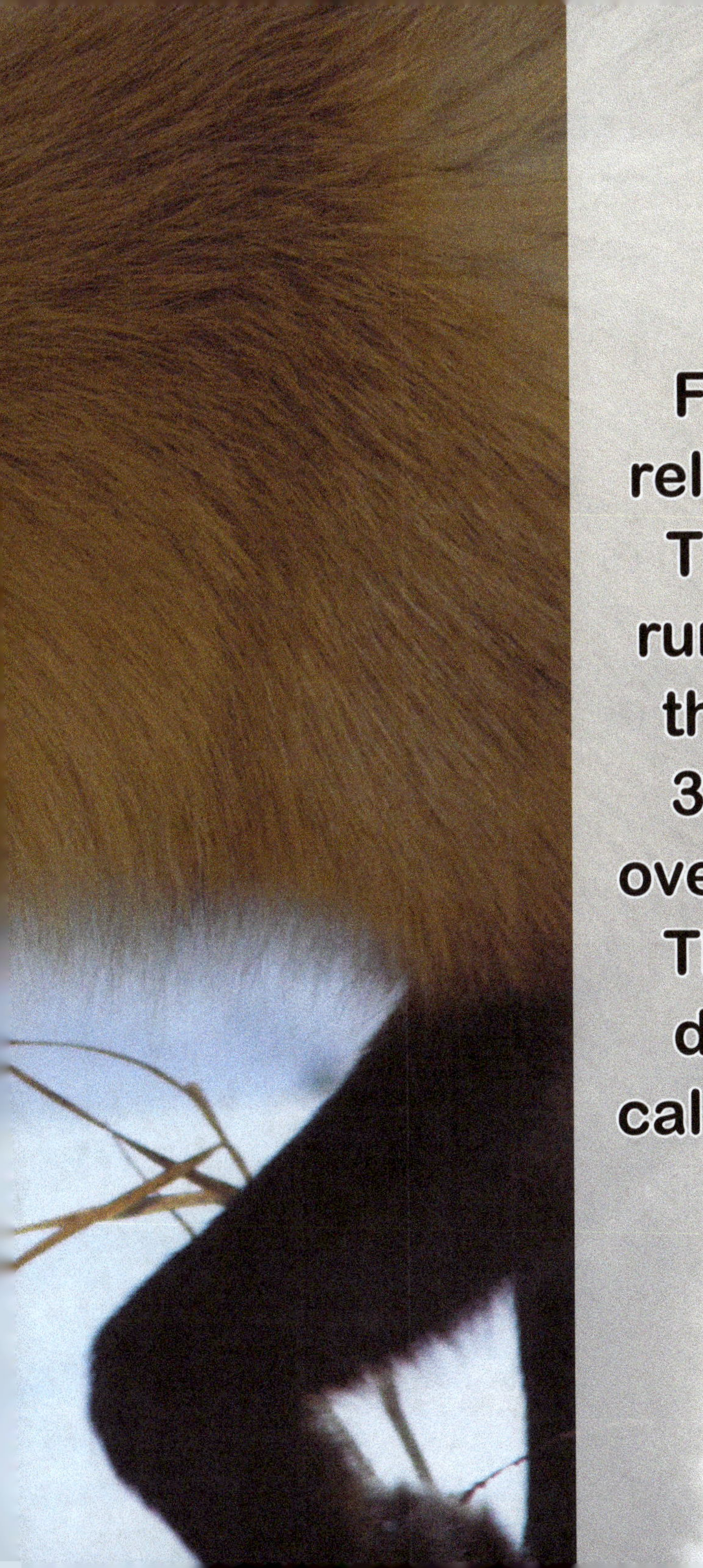

Foxes are distant relatives of the wolf. They are also fast runners. Amazingly, they can run up to 30 miles per hour over short distances. They can make 28 different types of calls to communicate with others.

HYENAS. Hyenas look like both dogs and cats, but they are from the Hyaenidae family. They are large carnivores, but they come in different sizes. They come in four types: spotted, brown, striped, and the aardwolf.

Hyenas are carnivores. They hunt for themselves, and also try to steal what other animals, like lions, have killed. The spotted hyenas are the largest of the hyena family. They are the most numerous among the four types. They produce strange sounds. That is why a spotted hyena is often called the laughing hyena.

The aardwolf is the smallest hyena, and only grows up to 20 inches length. Female hyenas are larger and more dominant than the males. Hyenas are nocturnal. They hunt at night and they are also scavengers.

Hyenas are
sometimes
characterized
as cannibals, for
they may eat other
hyenas. Their
greatest enemies
are lions and
hunting dogs.

These animals are
our companions here
on Earth. They are
parts of creation;
hence they have to be
loved and protected.

Visit
BABY PROFESSOR
EDUCATION KIDS
www.BabyProfessorBooks.com
to download Free Baby Professor eBooks
and view our catalog of new and exciting
Children's Books